Awakening MINDS

First published in 2022 by Leaping Hare Press,
an imprint of The Quarto Group.
The Old Brewery, 6 Blundell Street
London, N7 9BH,
United Kingdom
T (0)20 7700 6700
www.Quarto.com

Design © 2022 Quarto
Text © 2022 David J. Wallace

A catalogue record for this book is available from the
British Library.

ISBN 978-0-7112-7250-7
Ebook ISBN 978-0-7112-7251-4

10 9 8 7 6 5 4 3 2 1

Illustrations by Gabrielle Mabazza

Printed in China

MIX
Paper from
responsible sources
FSC® C016973

Awakening MINDS

10 LIFE LESSONS FOR A CONSCIOUS CULTURE

Illustrations by
Gabrielle Mabazza

DR. DAVID J. WALLACE

CONTENTS

"ULTIMATELY, IN ORDER
TO CREATE A CONSCIOUS
CULTURE, WE NEED TO BUILD
AN INFRASTRUCTURE OF PEACE,
LOVE, AND LIBERATION."

HOW TO USE THIS BOOK

This book features 10 chapters, each one dedicated to a different life lesson that I've encountered and learned over time. Each chapter starts with an introduction to the basic concepts of the lesson, followed by a personal story of how I've either experienced situations that helped me develop an enduring understanding of the life lesson, or have heard of the lesson and applied it directly to my life. After this you will find a segment called "Making It Work," which helps you identify the tools you need to apply the concepts of the lesson to your own life.

Meditation, Mindfulness and Journaling

At the end of each chapter, you'll find meditation and mindfulness exercises with space for drawing; and journaling question prompts, with space for writing. Here's your opportunity to really think about and engage with what you've just read, and we've provided space to capture your thoughts. Ultimately, express yourself in the way that the spirit moves you, whether it's through meditation, journaling, drawing, even dancing or shouting, if you need it. This is your book and your space, use it how you see fit.

Here are some instructions to help you prepare for the meditation and mindfulness exercises:

1   Find a quiet, comfortable space. You can choose to sit down or lie down. Whatever is most comfortable for you.
2   Consider reading through all the prompts first, before engaging in the exercise.
3   Set a timer, then close your eyes, take some deep breaths and relax.
4   Run through each question in turn, letting your thoughts run freely.
5   When the timer goes off, take a few deep breaths, open your eyes and consider how you're feeling after completing the exercise.

Let's Try One Out

First, preview the title of each chapter. Then, close your eyes and take 10 minutes to think about what you're hoping to gain from reading this book. Pay close attention to your breathing, and make note when your breathing is accelerating and slowing down. After previewing the book, reflect on:

What excites you about the book?

What concerns do you have?

What do you need to help you monitor and regulate your emotions as you navigate through the book?

What tools can you adapt to help you navigate the book?

Take It To Heart

These 10 life lessons have played a role in shaping my soul, my consciousness, and my concept of self. Like you, I have experiences that have challenged my perception of myself, the world, and the people around me. However, in the absence of experiences and connecting experiences to the life lessons, I would feel at a loss. As you read this book, make a commitment to connect the dots of experiences to lessons.

Enjoy!

Peace, love, and liberation.

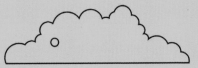

INTRODUCTION

Awakening Minds—a name born out of respect and reverence for my grandfather James Torrence Sr.'s journey through life.

I learned early on that my grandfather was forced out of school in the sixth grade to become a sharecropper and support his family. He grew up in the deep Jim Crow South, where it wasn't uncommon for Black people to be subjected to living and working conditions that eerily resembled the working conditions which our ancestors endured during and post chattel slavery. While laws had changed, conditions and beliefs stayed pretty stagnant.

My grandfather was a victim of systemic racism—never mind the fact that he didn't know what that meant, but he knew that there were systems that prevented him from accessing opportunities because of the color of his skin. Because he was forced out of school, he couldn't read. The opportunity of learning to read—once against the law and punishable by death—should now have been part of his civil rights, yet he still didn't benefit.

My grandfather's wisdom was uncompromising though, and people from the community of Belle Glade, Florida, leveraged that wisdom to help them reflect on and form life lessons of their own. My grandfather's love for gardening, his kindness and willingness to share is what attracted many people to him. People from the community would come to my grandparents' house for their fresh collard greens, cabbage, tomatoes, etc. The only form of payment that he would accept was to sit on the front porch and reflect on the journey called life.

When I went off to college, I leaned about the Ashanti or Asante people of Ghana, who developed Adinkra symbols to communicate aphorisms, or what I'd like to call "life lessons."

When developing the framework for this book, I thought about the term *Sankofa*, which means "to go back and get it," in other words, using knowledge gained in the past to guide your future. I used the knowledge, wisdom, and understanding of the world gleaned from my grandfather to develop these lessons. I watched and studied my grandfather over the years, and because of his journey, his triumphs, his challenges, and his wisdom, I am able to share these lessons with you.

These 10 life lessons can be read in any order that makes sense for you and your journey. Be warned, completion can be the enemy of process. Take your time, trust the process, and don't rush the process. Pick it up and put it down, and pick it back up. You may find that each time you read a chapter, you read it with a different perspective or understanding of the life lesson. That's okay.

Leverage the power of *Sankofa* to reflect on the past, understand the present, and prepare for the future—that's peace.

I need your help in creating a more just, kind, and conscious culture. As you're doing your work or after you've done your work, be sure to pull a friend, loved one, or colleague in. You may even decide to embark on this journey of building as a collective by reimagining your book club and cultivating a coalition of infrastructure builders who are all committed to taking this journey together—that's love.

Ultimately, in order to create a conscious culture, we need to build an infrastructure of peace, love, and liberation. There's a chance you may or may not agree with these lessons and how I've presented them. That's okay: Use this as a foundation to spark discourse about the lessons you've learned on your journey all while freeing yourself from the entrapment of the past—that's liberation.

LIFE LESSON

REJECTION

1

INTRODUCTION

Rejection is tough, and can sometimes feel like a blow to your ego, your consciousness, and your spirit. There are times when the rejection is so tough that it changes the shape of your soul. But, what we do with rejection is as important as the rejection itself.

For some of us, we allow that rejection to take over our lives, alter our behavior, and put us on a path of darkness and demise. Imagine that you really liked someone. You went on several dates with this person, and even started to develop feelings for them. One day, the person you're dating suddenly tells you that they're not interested in you. You get so upset that you head out for a night on the town, drink your life away, and find some random person to have sex with. You wouldn't normally hook up with a stranger, but the disappointment was so great that you spiraled out of control.

You continue this pattern of behavior, and convince yourself that this risky sexual behavior is your method of getting over your ex. The more people you meet, the more people you give your heart to. One day you realize that you're in a depression, and can't seem to get out of the sunken place. Damn rejection.

There's another way

For others, rejection is expected and accepted, therefore more time and energy are spent looking beyond the rejection rather than dwelling in the negative feelings associated with rejection. In the case above, the rejection is still the same and it still hurts, but rather than engaging in risky sexual behavior you spend time with your squad, talk about the situation for a bit, then start to think through all the things you're going to accomplish now that the situation has set sail. You also spend some time reflecting on the lessons you learned from that situation, like that your communication skills need to drastically improve.

That's one of the most critical parts of rejection—having the opportunity to reflect on what you learned about yourself from your involvement in the situation. You leave space for grief, but you enter every situation knowing that there's a risk of rejection, and recover from the rejection quicker and somewhat easier.

Onward and upward

A select few though understand the bigger picture about rejection and disappointment, and use rejection as a stepping stone to their next triumph or blessing. In the case above, after your night out with the squad, you decide that you're going to pursue that certification that you've always wanted. You use the rejection as an opportunity for personal development. Six months later, you've completed your certification and are ready for a promotion at work. One day your squad asks you, what made you go back to school for another certification? You smile, and share that suddenly closing a chapter on what you thought was going to be a long-term relationship gave you the vote of confidence, and time, to pursue something that you've wanted for years.

Blessings can be born of the biggest disappointment and greatest tragedies. We must, however, hold the space to process and reflect on those disappointments and tragedies, then look beyond them. How can you make sense of a situation? Reflect on how you showed up in that situation, and use this reflection to give you a sense of purpose.

TURNING REJECTION INTO A BLESSING

It took years for me to realize that my greatest blessings stemmed from my biggest disappointment—my father rejecting me because of my sexuality.

Initially, I allowed the rejection to take up too much space in my life. During my sophomore and junior years of college, I experimented with drugs. I fell in love with the party scene in Atlanta, going out most nights of the week. I was angry. I got into several fights at bars, had a short temper, and struggled to open up in romantic relationships. My college grades suffered, and there were moments when I simply wanted to give up. Looking back, I realize that I had the ability to mask my emotions and experiences with ease, which some would refer to symptoms of high-functional depression. I wanted to feel accepted, so I engaged in things that I wouldn't normally do because I was seeking the attention and approval of my sexuality from others.

I wish I had known more about mental health services back then. I remember enrolling into a psychology of meditation course that changed my outlook about rejection. One day, the professor asked us to close our eyes and think about something that had caused us grief. She then asked: "What would it mean for you to turn that grief into some good?" She instructed us to take the next 10 minutes, breathing, and creating space in our brain to grapple with that question.

Connections

I grappled, drifted, and even fought the idea of making good out of my awful situation. Then suddenly, I found myself at peace. I began to draw connections between my erratic behavior and the causes of me exhibiting those behaviors.

I realized that I was depressed, angry, and was lashing out every chance I got. If I continued down that path, I could have found myself in trouble, seriously hurt, and not completing college. So, I decided to make a change by recommitting myself to my spiritual practices, and exploring meditation more in depth. What would it mean for me to fully accept the rejection of my father, and use that energy for some good?

Because of his rejection, I set out on a journey to prove to myself that I didn't need his love and acknowledgment to make it in life. Senior year, I had two goals: finish college strong, and land a teaching job in New York. I was determined to have a reset, including leaving Atlanta. Like everyone else, I continued to experience rejection throughout my life. However, the blows got easier to receive as I would anticipate the plausibility of rejection, and also push myself not to dwell in disappointment for too long. I would double up on meditation when I experienced rejection, as it served as an opportunity for me to reflect on the steps I needed to take to recover from the rejection.

Silver linings

Over a decade later, I found myself hit with another major rejection. I interviewed for a promotion at work that would elevate me to a leadership position, but I was not granted the role. However, I was given the opportunity to take on managing partnerships for my company and serve on the senior leadership team, which was still considered a promotion. I hesitantly accepted the role and, within six months, I was interviewing for a leadership role that would require me to relocate to New Orleans, and oversee the entire region.

I couldn't help but reflect on how the role I initially wanted didn't work out for me and how the new role was a bigger and better opportunity.

"TO BE CONTENT WITH THE
POSSIBILITY OF REJECTION
IS TO BE AT PEACE WITH
THE OUTCOME, REGARDLESS
OF YOUR DESIRES."

MAKING IT WORK

Once we accept the fact that rejection is inevitable, we unlock a part of our spirit that allows us to enter any situation with a level of peace that we couldn't reach prior to acknowledging rejection is possible.

To be content with the possibility of rejection is to be at peace with the outcome, regardless of your desires. The disappointment that you feel when being rejected is a normal feeling, and we should provide space in our lives to process it. What we can't do is dwell in disappointment.

You have to push yourself to look beyond the disappointment because your blessing could arise out of the very thing that disappointed you. I will often say to myself, "Well that didn't work out because something better is on its way."

One has to ask, is it possible to manifest these blessings because you were rejected? In the absence of the rejection, would you be able to secure that next promotion?

MEDITATIONS ON REJECTION

5 Minutes

Close your eyes, and think about a time when you were rejected. Pay close attention to your breathing.

If you visualize an image while meditating, draw it here

5 Minutes

Now think about what came after the rejection. Did you accept it? Did your behavior change? For the good or the bad? If you could do it all over again, what would you do? What would it have meant to take that rejection and do some good?

REFLECTIONS ABOUT REJECTION

Think about something you're looking forward to.

What are the possible outcomes?

Which outcome would be considered a rejection?

How will you respond if the outcome is, in fact, a rejection?

How will you respond if the outcome is, in fact, not a rejection?

LIFE LESSON

INTELLECTUAL EXILE

2

INTRODUCTION

What thoughts come to mind when you think about intellectual exile? Have you ever been in a place or situation where you felt completely out of place, ostracized, oppressed? Though we're conditioned to be socialized beings, there are times where we find ourselves mentally, physically, and emotionally detached from a place.

For example, perhaps you grew up in a small town and never felt a true connection to that town? Or you work for a company where there's a misalignment between your personal values and principles and what the company represents. Or maybe your identity markers, such as race, age, class, are the only identity markers represented in a space.

Intellectual exile. You're often in a place, but not of that place.

The privilege of the majority

Some people have the privilege of navigating life, without ever feeling like an outsider—ostracized or oppressed. Exile is foreign to them because they are part of the dominant culture or responsible for creating spaces that are deemed exclusive and reserved for a certain class. This could be circumstantial, or by design.

There are systems and institutions that create this dynamic, and when those systems and institutions are penetrated by the "other" there's often a cultural war that commences. The perfect homogenous synergy is interrupted, and opportunity for chaos ensues.

Have you ever? ...

If you've gotten this far, and are still wondering if you've ever experienced intellectual exile or have caused someone else to experience it, here are some examples.

Imagine

... being the first Black person to attend an Ivy League institution designed by and for White people.

... what it was like for the first woman to land a job at a Fortune 500 company that was dominated by men.

... growing up gay, and not feeling comfortable discussing your sexuality because you're surrounded by heterosexuals with homophobic mindsets.

... being the only Black male teacher at your school, that serves Black and Brown kids, dominated by White women.

... growing up experiencing anxiety every time you're required to speak out loud at school, and not having the tools to communicate your feelings with others.

... working for a company, and not being able to express your religious beliefs for fear of judgment or retaliation.

Some of us have the luxury of never having to experience these examples. For others, they are a testament to their experiences or even barely graze the surface of their experiences.

SOCIETAL BIASES

Elementary school is a pivotal time in our lives ... and it is also when gender and identity norms are taught at an accelerated pace. It is as if society deemed elementary school the place where you unknowingly learn about systemic biases.

Now I know part of my understanding of the world was developed prior to entering grade school, but let's face it, elementary school taught us a lot about the way society is "supposed" to operate when it comes to class, race, disability, gender lines ....

I was directly or indirectly taught that girls wore pink, played with dolls, showed their admiration for a boy by being mean to him, and, most importantly, liked boys; women were nurses, teachers, cooked and prepared meals for the family, and did dishes. I was also taught that boys didn't cry, had to be tough, wore blue and/or green, played sports, and had to have a girl crush. White men were firefighters, scientists, doctors, and shaped America. I still remember the pictures used to teach vocabulary words.

Playing along

So here I was, an elementary school kid who was aware of his differences. Of course, I played into hetero-norms to fit in with the popular crowd, confessing my girl crushes to the boys on the playground, asking girls out with the "Do you like me, yes, no, maybe" folded paper, beating up any boy that tried to flex on me. Yep, that was me, living through intellectual exile. I was aware that I was different, but that the folks around me might not have the capacity to understand my differences.

Finding my way out

Fortunately, total exile, in regard to my sexuality, didn't last a lifetime. I found others who were like me in middle school, and even discovered a close cousin was like me.

Despite still having to navigate intellectual exile in certain spaces, I found my tribe along the way in high school, college, and my career. I found best friends who walked similar paths to mine, and who are now more like brothers than friends. My maternal brother and I have become closer over the years, and he stands firmly as an ally for the LGBTQIA community.

I've also outreached to other men who walk a similar path as I do to mentor, coach, and advise. I then started to share my experiences navigating spaces places that felt like intellectual exile, all in hopes of inspiring others.

"BUILD A TRIBE ...
CAST THE NET WIDE."

MAKING IT WORK

Over the years, I developed ways to cope with intellectual exile. I hope these will help you as well.

Build

The first, and most important recommendation, is to build a tribe. Build your tribe of individuals who will support you through challenging times, who will celebrate you when you're winning, and lend a helping hand when you're losing at life. It goes beyond that friend who will share your success stories on Instagram.

Push yourself to build a tribe that shares your identity markers, and ones that don't. After all, you don't want to fall victim to echo chambers, as we all deserve to experience and learn from diverse perspectives.

Widen

My second recommendation is to cast the net wide. At first, it was hard being the only Black male classroom teacher. None of my tribe members shared my experience. I researched support organizations and I also started to meet other Black Male Educators across the country. From casting my net wide, I've built life-long friendships, partnerships, and camaraderie with guys who I have a ton of respect for. When I struggled to find the tailored support that I needed, I didn't give up: I widened my search.

MEDITATIONS ON INTELLECTUAL EXILE

5 Minutes

Close your eyes, and think about a period in your life. Have you ever experienced intellectual exile? Or have you created conditions to cause others to experience intellectual exile? Pay close attention to your breathing.

✏ **If you visualize an image while meditating, draw it here**

5 Minutes

Now think more deeply about that experience. What did it feel like? How did you cope with it? Are there feelings you're harboring that deserve to be let go?

REFLECTIONS ABOUT INTELLECTUAL EXILE

Think about another time when you've experienced intellectual exile or caused someone else to experience it.

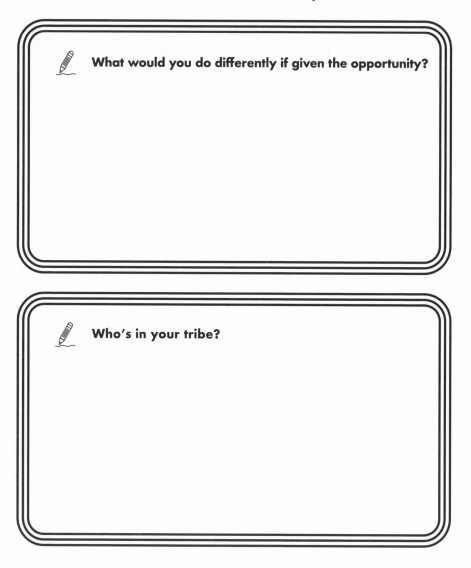

🖉 **What would you do differently if given the opportunity?**

🖉 **Who's in your tribe?**

✏️ **Is there additional soul work that you need to do to build your tribe?**

✏️ **How might this tribe help you?**

LIFE LESSON

3

INTROSPECTION

INTRODUCTION

In the absence of reflection, the soul runs shallow. We're constantly met with our reflection throughout the day, while brushing our teeth, out the car window, or taking that next selfie for social media. When the pandemic hit, many of us saw our reflections on virtual calls.

In fact, our physical reflection has become so prevalent that we've stopped considering who's looking back at us. We've also become more focused on how our reflection looks to others. But what happens when you stare in the mirror six seconds longer than you normally would? What do you see? Is it that we've stopped reflecting on experiences because we're tired of looking at ourselves? Or is it that we're afraid to confront what stares back at us in the mirror. We lack depth in the absence of reflection.

To be reflective is to give space for thinking and to build awareness and understanding of the world around you. To be introspective is to provide space to consider your emotions while also thinking about moments or experiences. I consider reflection the first step before introspection. In other words, you can't consider your emotions without considering the experience.

A work example

Let's say that you've just had an interview for a work promotion. Afterward, you find yourself walking to your car, asking yourself, "Did I answer the questions clearly? Did I provide concrete examples? Was I clear in my responses?" You might even wonder, "Did I wear the appropriate tie or dress for the interview?" We're conditioned to evaluate our performance regardless of situation or circumstances.

But to be reflective, we might ask ourselves "How was the experience interviewing for the role? Where did I excel in the interview? Where did I struggle or feel challenged in the interview?" Those questions get at the heart of your experience, and create space for you to answer deeply.

To be introspective, one might ask "How do I feel about the overall interview experience? How did I feel at different points in the interview? Were there moments when my heart rate increased or slowed down? What was my breathing like during the interview?" These questions require a deeper level of analysis and understanding of the mind, body, and spirit. Connecting the experiences to the emotions can provide a new level of clarity.

Personal lives

These reflection and introspection questions can also be answered after a personal experience. For example, you meet someone in an online dating app and after some time you decide to take things to go on your first date. You're incredibly nervous, but loosen up once you've sipped a few cocktails and dove into a conversation about your life's purpose. Dinner lasts for hours, with interesting discussions. You're driving home from dinner, smiling because you've both agreed to see each other again. Why?

This is where the reflection and introspection questions are pivotal. You want to provide space to think about why you like someone, and what characteristics drew you to them. You also want to consider how that person made you feel on the inside. Do you think they contributed to your nerves being calmed or was it the alcohol? How did you show up to dinner? Were you presenting as your authentic self or someone you thought they wanted to date?

It is important to do that type of reflection so that you're aware of how you may have been perceived at the dinner— you can then harness the energy that you were most proud of for the next date, and change the things you didn't like at the next date.

WHAT IF IT'S NOT GOOD NEWS?

The two previous examples were seemingly positive experiences. But what if you experience something traumatic? Is that event or experience worthy of the same depth of reflection and introspection? I think that, in fact, it's even more important.

Several years ago my grandfather was diagnosed with colon cancer, and my world felt like it was turned upside down. I was in my third year teaching in New York, and was living the dream. But I put all this on hold, and moved to Miami to step in as a caregiver. After a year, my grandpa's cancer went into remission and there was hope that he'd continue to lead a healthy life. I returned to New York. Once back, I seemed to navigate New York differently. I felt a greater sense of purpose and calling to help people, on a larger scale. I switched my career to higher education, training, and developing teachers.

Within six months, my grandpa's cancer returned. I questioned my decision to leave Miami so quickly. Six months on from this, he passed away and my mental health suffered. I fell into a depression, beating myself up about leaving him too early. But I began to attend meditation classes, and journaled at night. I began to reflect on the moments I shared with him the year before, each moment bringing a smile to my face. I also considered how I felt during those moments, such as throwing him a surprise birthday party or celebrating the Fourth of July with a family cookout. There was nothing more beautiful than seeing my grandpa smile. I remember asking myself: How was the experience?

It was hard to drop everything and move to Miami. There was a level of uncertainty about my grandpa's cancer treatment that made it hard to remain optimistic. The move also put a strain on my relationship. Despite the odds, I remained committed to my grandpa, my graduate studies, and my relationship.

MAKING IT WORK

In order to be introspective and reflective, the first thing you must do is create space in your life for the depth of thinking or mental work to occur. Too often we're so consumed with the next thing in our schedule, that we forget to pencil in this critical work. So the first thing you need to do is commit to creating space for reflection and introspection.

Secondly, develop a set of questions. Feel free to use the ones posed throughout this chapter, to embark on the experience of reflection and introspection. You'll find that the more space you create for this critical work, the more your mind and body will be at ease, regardless of the outcome. In my case, I asked myself three questions to learn from my experience of balancing my career with my family obligations.

Where did I thrive or excel?

I excelled in graduate school, and led a school through tough times academically. My relationship with my family and connection with my grandpa grew stronger. My personality type of commander thrived during this period, and it felt good to keep things in order.

Where did I struggle or feel challenged?

It was challenging to build social connections in Miami. Outside of the friends I made at work, there were very few opportunities for me to meet new people, and I was also living back at home with my mom and little sister. Although my mom gave me the space to be an adult, there was still that feeling of being back at home. My desire to respect my mother proved to be a barrier for my ability to build deep social connections. I don't regret it though.

What is the biggest lesson I learned?

I am able to step boldly into decision-making, which has caused me to regret very little in my life. I lead with love, and love everything that I lead. Humility is a key to longevity.

MEDITATIONS ON INTROSPECTION

5 Minutes

Think about a moment in your life today, yesterday, or even this past week. Once you have that moment, close your eyes. Think about that moment, paying close attention to what pops up in your mind. What was that moment like? How did you show up at that moment? What was the outcome? Are you satisfied with the outcome? Pay close attention to your breathing.

If you visualize an image while meditating, draw it here

5 Minutes

How do you feel about that moment? How did you respond to that moment? Are you satisfied with that moment? If you could, would you change anything about that moment?

REFLECTIONS ABOUT INTROSPECTION

Consider a challenging situation that you experienced.

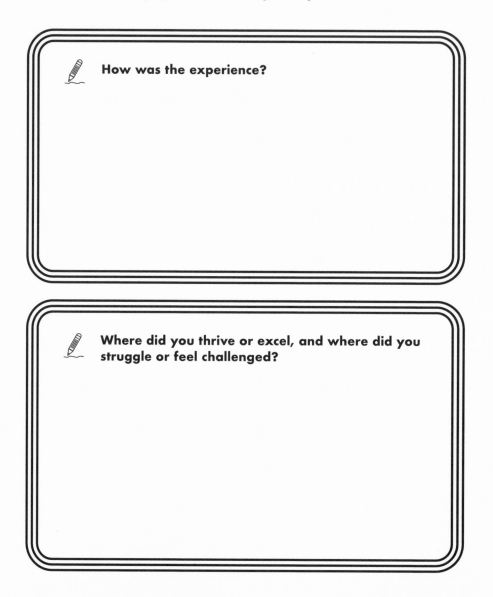

How was the experience?

Where did you thrive or excel, and where did you struggle or feel challenged?

How do you feel about the experience overall,
and at different points within it?

What is the biggest lesson learned from
that experience?

LIFE
LESSON

PURPOSE

4

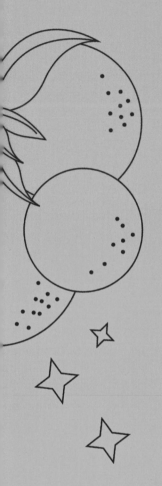

INTRODUCTION

You can't plant the seed of hope and neglect to water with action. Think about a recent desire or thing that you hoped for. What steps did you take to make that desire come true?

Too often, we set goals, desires, dreams, and intentions with little to no effort put into making those things come true. It's not necessarily our fault. We've been conditioned from birth to desire. That's universal. What's not universal is the energy, willingness, and steps taken to achieve the desire, want, craving, or need. That's learned behavior acquired by your caregivers, their beliefs and values, your developing consciousness, and your environment.

When you were a child, you likely learned the difference between instant and delayed gratification. For example, a 10-year old requests the latest game console, and their parents go out and buy it: Instant gratification. But some children grow up with the expectation from their parents that they must earn their rewards. Another 10-year old might be instead assigned an expectation, such as completing a series of chores. They would work toward achieving that goal, and would be eventually rewarded with their initial desires—the game console gives them delayed gratification.

Other kids grow up asking but never receiving, which creates a window for different outcomes. A child could grow up asking and never receiving, therefore finding the means to accomplish things on their own. This creates another window of opportunity, as the child could take the path of hard work, perseverance, and eventually achieve success in life or they could travel down a more negative path by becoming a criminal who steals, lies, and cheats to get what they want.

A child could also grow up, with a similar experience but slightly different conditioning that would lead to them never asking for things, never asking for help, never learning how to work hard towards a goal, and ultimately being okay with never having what they might want. Fast forward to adulthood and that manifests itself with characteristics of laziness, mediocrity, and self-defeated and depleted thinking.

Human development is complex, and complicated by many factors, such as upbringing, environment, personality type in development, and the list goes on. I don't want to oversimplify the connection between childhood development and the impact that it has on adult development, but there is an association. In my experience, I've encountered adults who are goal driven, persevere through challenging situations, and operate with a sense of purpose. I've also encountered adults who lack the ability to set goals, whether small or large, let alone achieve them. And there are some adults who expect the world to revolve around them, have rarely experienced failure, and therefore find it difficult to navigate a role in which their parental influence is minimized or diminished. I refer to these people as lost, out of touch with the real word, and drowning in privilege. If you've always been given what you want, then do you lack desire and determination? I would say no, but if you've never had to work or prove yourself for something, your "purpose bucket" might run shallow.

One thing to note—mental health can impact where you fall along that spectrum of purpose in adulthood, but for those who are not experiencing struggles with mental health, making the connections between how you were conditioned to think about desires as a child can unlock a deeper understanding of how you show up as an adult, particularly as you're trying to establish a sense of purpose. In other words, experiences from childhood impact the amount of energy, work, and effort we put into achieving goals as adults.

FINDING FUEL TO FIND PURPOSE

I grew up in a single family home—my mom worked during the day and completed her graduate studies in the evening. My siblings and I spent a lot of time at our grandparents' house. One day in sophomore year I came home from school and my grandfather had a stack of mail for me to read. I never understood why he would ask family members to read things for him. I asked him why he always wait for me to read his mail.

He responded: "Son, I can't read. I didn't have the opportunity to finish school like my kids did, and like you are. When I was in the sixth grade, I had to stop going to school to work on a farm and support my family. Even when I was in school, the teachers didn't really care about me, so your grandpa has to depend on you all to help me understand the world around me. This is also why your grandma and I worked so hard to put our five kids through school, so that you all won't have to experience what I experienced."

His response caused me to drift into deep thought. At first I was saddened by what he shared, but it made me realize that although slavery in America had ended, the effects of it continued to impact Black people in a systemic way. My grandpa persevered through the systemic barriers that were placed before him, and still worked hard to provide for his family. Though proud of his ability to navigate a racist system, I was determined to interrupt that, so I decided to become a teacher. I volunteered at the local elementary school through a grow-your-own teaching program, and had the opportunity to be excused from high school to take college classes.

Every step after that moment led me to my purpose. Eventually, I had the opportunity to land a summer teaching internship in New York. My grandpa's story was fueling my sense of purpose. I told myself, if I could impact one child in this world, to help them see themselves not as what society has deemed them to be but what they are destined to be, then I'll feel vindicated in my decision to pursue education.

Since then, my purpose has evolved but I remain fueled by my grandpa's story. Each opportunity that presents itself is a chance for me to play a role in disrupting a system that has wronged my grandpa, and so many other Black people.

Although I discovered my sense of purpose in high school, I was also conditioned to work towards my goals and desires. My mom would reward me with most things I asked for, but it also came with a charge or a goal. For example, I would always ask for the latest game console or sneakers. Her response was always "you can have _____ if you do _____." At the time, I didn't realize that she was conditioning me that I must work hard for things that I earned, that I would have a greater sense of self if I rightly earned something as opposed to taking it or receiving it without any effort.

I also witnessed my mother struggle for a better life for her family. She taught me that while conditions may not always be favorable, you can still try to flip those conditions. Within a matter of years, she went from being considered part of the lower class to middle class, based on her job and income. I know for some, their conditions are far too great for that to change as quickly as we did, but I have to think that drive, determination, and sense of purpose helped her accomplish that.

"IT IS IMPORTANT THAT
WE ACKNOWLEDGE THE STEPS
BETWEEN THE WANT AND THE
OUTCOME. THAT IS WHERE
THE REAL WORK HAPPENS."

MAKING IT WORK

Our understanding of "purpose" can be traced back to our upbringing, and how we've been conditioned to think about our sense of self, our sense of others, and our sense of the world. Self-determination and self-fulfilling prophecy that dictate our paths to achieving our purpose, our wants, our desires.

It is important that we acknowledge the steps between the want and the outcome. That is where the real work happens. When we express a desire, want, or need, we also need to invest the time to do the work. That requires setting realistic goals and charting a path towards achieving them. Let's say that you've discovered that your purpose in life is to help others, and you've decided that you'll achieve that by becoming a teacher. Some realistic goals might be setting a timeline for yourself to earn the degree required to teach, committing to studying for the certification exams, and ultimately applying for a teaching role.

It may also mean finding ways to navigate the conditions in which we exist, and working to reduce or eliminate barriers that stand in the way of achieving one's true purpose in life. In the case of the previous example, one might experience barriers to becoming certified. For example, certification exams are incredibly difficult to pass and costly. One way to navigate or reduce the barrier is to seek out financial assistance from the state or local agencies. Another way to reduce barriers is to seek out study materials and others who are studying for the exam and create a study group. Ultimately, zoom out and ask yourself "what's getting in the way of me achieving my purpose?" Then create an action plan or path forward.

MEDITATIONS ON PURPOSE

10 Minutes

Close your eyes, and think about the principles and values that guide your life. Do those principles and values connect to what you're currently doing in your life professionally and personally? What's your purpose?

If you visualize an image while meditating, draw it here

10 Minutes

Close your eyes and think about the conditions you're currently navigating. Are those conditions serving as barriers to you achieving your purpose? Are the conditions just right for you to achieve your purpose? What do you need more of or less of during this time?

REFLECTIONS ABOUT PURPOSE

Think about why you are here at this moment in time.

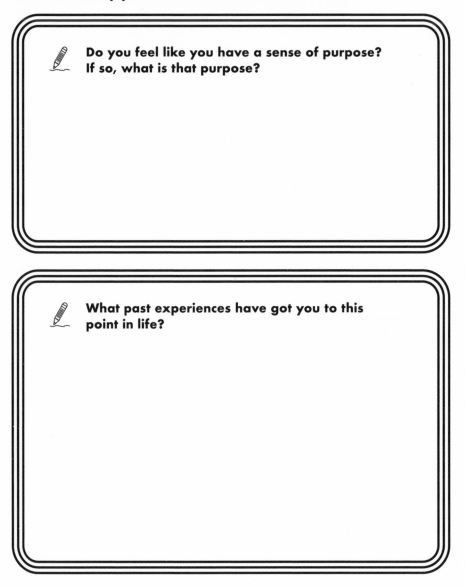

🖊 **Do you feel like you have a sense of purpose? If so, what is that purpose?**

🖊 **What past experiences have got you to this point in life?**

How do those past experiences connect to your future goals?

How do your future goals connect to your sense of purpose?

LIFE LESSON

SELF-RESPECT

5

INTRODUCTION

To have self-respect is to operate with a sense of pride, honor, and dignity. It also means to have a sense of self-worth, value, and reverence for yourself, your experiences, your talent, your mind, your body, and ultimately your spirit.

Too often, as a kid I heard adults say "believe in yourself", which I took as a precursor for having respect for yourself. To "believe in yourself" not only means to consider the things you can do, it also means to refrain from doing things that don't align with who you believe yourself to be. To "believe in yourself" is to recognize that we're all unique, and that our lived, learned, and labored experiences make the journey called life an oasis of opportunities and challenges. It is through those experiences that we develop a sense of self, values, and principles that guide our life. That makes us uniquely qualified to tell our own story, because there's no one that has the same lived experience as you.

But what happens when you fail to believe in yourself, your values, and violate your self-respect? You disrespect yourself every time you say yes when you want to say no. Peer pressure can often force you to set aside your beliefs and values in order to fit into a social setting. It causes us to disrespect our personal beliefs and values all for the sake of fitting in, and being liked.

As we progress through life there are some people who make a conscious decision to deny societal pressures, regardless of the circumstance. There are others who find it more challenging to discern societal pressures because of the setting and conditions in which the pressure is occurring. For example, in workplaces, peer pressure oftentimes takes the form of management pressure or corporate pressure. People are asked to do things, such as taking on projects without proper compensation or support, and they take them on because they believe that it's a path to their next promotion or strong rankings on their performance review. Opportunities to practice self-respect are limited in work environments because there's an inherent fear that if you say no, your future is jeopardized.

But what if we became more comfortable saying no to things because we "believe" that our worthiness and value is not being honored? When you operate with a sense of self-respect or self-worth, you're able to lead life considering your personal principles and values, and you're able to step boldly into opportunities believing that your experiences make you uniquely qualified for those experiences. You're also able to say "yes" and "no" to things that align and don't align to your values. To have self-respect is also to be keenly aware of how your thoughts, actions, and words can have a profound impact on others. Social and emotional intelligence lives in the arena of self-respect.

STRUGGLING TO SAY NO

Not long ago, I was approached by a national organization to lead a keynote speech on the importance and impact of Juneteenth.

At this time, I was in communication with the Vice President of Human Resources. He shared with me that this was the first time that the organization would be embarking on a celebration of Juneteenth, and having me as the keynote speaker would grant me exposure to the organization. This exposure, he said, could be beneficial with regard to future consulting opportunities. The VP then asked me for a speaking rate for the 15-minute keynote speech, which I provided. To my surprise, his response stated that he was surprised by the proposed rate, that he'd had a rate in mind significantly lower. I was tempted to take the lower rate, almost convinced by the opportunity for exposure. It took all my energy to formulate a response to him.

Ultimately, I declined the opportunity, and shared with the VP of HR that, given the gravity of the content, the number of employees, and the timing of the request, my rate was equitable. I wished them the best of luck in pursuit of their programming. Although I never heard back from him, I again questioned my decision, though I felt a sense of pride declining the opportunity.

Why did I have a habit of questioning decisions that related to assessing my self-worth and value? The answer is, I experienced psychological oppression. People with power tend to cause those without power or in less powerful positions to experience psychological oppression. When you question your decisions, you question your value, you question your self-worth, and ultimately you question your self-respect. So in order to combat psychological oppression, I've started telling myself "I made this decision because I respect myself. I made this decision for myself, and only myself."

MAKING IT WORK

Societal pressures, which show up in the form of family pressure, peer pressure, corporate pressure, etc., can have a lasting effect on our self-respect. It is important that we consider these pressures when assessing our ability to make decisions for ourselves. In some instances, it may be easier to say no, in other instances you may feel that you have no other option but to say yes—we must call attention to those perilous areas where decision making is more challenging, deceiving, and could cause harm to our psychological safety.

As you consider your decision-making power, also consider the implications of those decisions. For example, what would saying no mean for you personally? What would it mean for the person or entity that you declined? It is important to think about the potential outcomes of the decision as you make the decision. Personally, doing this level of critical thinking boosts my confidence, as I prepare to deliver the "no." There's no better feeling than saying "no" with conviction, because you've done the work necessary to prepare yourself for any possible outcome of that decision.

MEDITATIONS ON SELF-RESPECT

5 Minutes

Take a moment to think about your concept of self. What does self-worth mean to you? How do you demonstrate that you're worthy of respect?

If you visualize an image while meditating, draw it here

5 Minutes

Next, think about a mantra that you can chant for the next 5 minutes by completing this sentence: "I am worthy of ..." Now I want you to think about what you will not sacrifice, and add that to your chant: "I will not sacrifice my ____ because I'm worthy of _____."

REFLECTIONS ABOUT SELF-RESPECT

Consider a decision that you've made that caused you to sacrifice your self-respect.

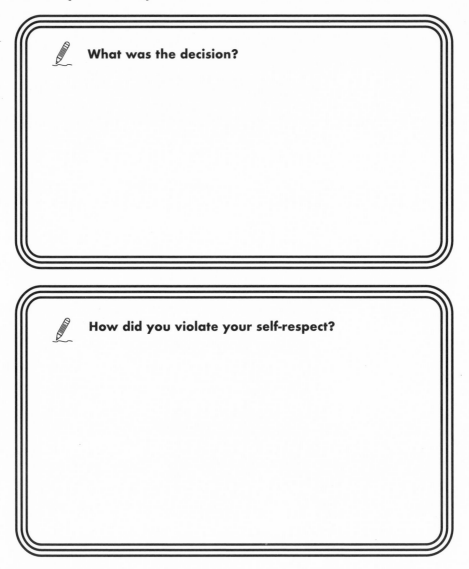

✏️ **What was the decision?**

✏️ **How did you violate your self-respect?**

✏️ **What difference do you think it would have made if that decision had been rooted in self-respect?**

✏️ **If you could do it all over again, what would you do differently?**

LIFE LESSON
LESSON
FORGIVENESS

6

INTRODUCTION

I wish life better prepared us for disappointment, heartache, and pain. Of course, one would have to experience these things in order to truly be prepared for them, but is there a way to lessen the blow?

Maybe, maybe not. I once heard my mom say, you better live your life freely because one day you'll fall in love and you'll get your heart broken. It'll be one of the worst pains you've ever experienced, it'll be hard to recover from it, but you'll have the experiences of living life to fall back on and those experiences will help you recover from the disappointment.

Experiencing pain or trauma at the hands of another person can have lasting and damaging effects on your mental psyche. There's a reason that post-traumatic stress disorder (PTSD) exists, and it doesn't only come from going to war. Experiencing trauma changes the shape of your soul. People have even lost themselves in the wake of trauma and pain. At one point or another, I was one of those people. In order to combat the pain, one must be willing to forgive the person who caused the pain. You can move on from the person, but without forgiveness, you'll never move on from the pain.

I wished that my mom had also shared that forgiveness was key to fully recovering and moving on with your life. Sure, I was able to leverage my lived, learned, and labored experiences to aid in recovering from heartache, but that feeling of resentment and being unsettled lingered for years. I wish I could have told her that forgiveness was a pivotal part of her recovering from the pain my father caused her, and the pain other men in her life caused her who came before and after my father.

For if she had forgiven them, I truly believe that she'd lead a life that was free of the remnants of heartache, disappointment, and pain. Forgiveness doesn't mean that you have to forget the trauma caused by the pain. It does however, set you on a path to recovering quicker and moving on with life free of baggage.

When you fail to forgive, you allow the person, the trauma, the pain, to live rent free in your mind, body, and soul. Failing to forgive also gives that person, pain, and trauma power and control over your emotions.

In order to chart a path to recovery, forgiveness is key.

FORGIVENESS HEALS ALL

During my sophomore year at Morehouse College, I met a guy who would change my love, heartbreak, and forgiveness, forever. I was out one night at a club with my friends, when I got talking to an attractive man named "B." That night, he shared with me that he was newly single and not really looking for anything serious. Naively, I became captivated by his words and the thought of us having fun together. I obliged and shared that I, too, wasn't looking for anything serious.

Our lives soon merged. Within a matter of two months, we went from being friends, to partners, to saying "I love you." I felt like myself again and I thought that I'd gotten over the depression from my dad disowning me, while in reality I had found a beautiful bandaid to cover the wound.

During the winter, I went to Egypt for 21 days on a school-sponsored expedition. Our limited communication caused me to miss him dearly. When I returned home, B was different. We continued to date for several months, until one day I got a call from his ex-boyfriend, who shared that while I was away, they had rekindled their relationship and that B had told him that he would break things off with me. My heart sank.

When I approached B, he initially denied the whole thing and became very upset. We didn't speak for a couple weeks, but one day, he called and asked to meet in the park. When I got there, he began to cry and beg for my forgiveness. He stated that everything his ex shared was true, that they'd rekindled their relationship while I was gone, but when I came back he began to have second thoughts. He shared that he was torn, loved us both, and that we each brought something different to his life.

I told B that I forgave him, and that I hoped that he'd find some closure with this situation. I told him that I didn't have the energy to compete for his attention, and that when we became involved with each other I knew I was taking a risk, as his rebound. I thanked him for the past eight months, and told him that I wouldn't harbor any negative feelings against him. At that time, I couldn't fault him for his infidelity, because he didn't love himself enough to free himself from the pain that his ex caused him. He was repeating the very behaviors that I witnessed. There's a saying that "hurt people hurt people." I was determined not to continue that cycle.

Several months later, I ran into B's ex-boyfriend at a party. He greeted me with open arms and made note of how good I looked. He shared that he was single and asked if we could grab dinner together, to maybe start over. This was a terrible idea.

I told him that some chapters are never worth reopening, and that was one of them. I wished him the best in life, and never saw him again. This was confirmation that forgiving B helped me to let go of the pain.

Since then, I've forgiven every person who has caused me harm, and worked to see every experience as a learning experience. I often ask myself, "What would it mean for you to completely let go of the wall and surrender?" While I'm not always great at answering the question, I know that forgiveness is key to unlocking and releasing pain.

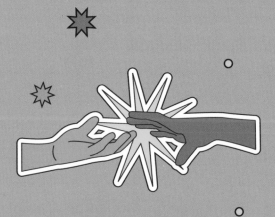

**"THE GREATER
THE PAIN,
THE GREATER
THE RECOVERY."**

MAKING IT WORK

When people have wronged you, it has a lasting effect on how you continue to show up in the world.

For some, this disappointment is so damaging that it not only compromises their psychological safety but it also leads to mental health issues, such as depression. For others, those damaging effects show up as barriers or walls created by the victim. They are reluctant to be vulnerable, let others in, and truly get to know someone out of fear of being hurt again. Years of disappointment and pain can cause barriers that are so great that the victim loses sight of who they are as a person. The pain is so great and so deep, that the victim doesn't even know where to begin the healing process.

It is important that we assess the impact of pain on our mind, body, and spirit. The greater the pain, the greater the recovery. In the absence of forgiveness, pain lives on through action and inaction. We've all experienced pain, but we all haven't dealt with the pain.

MEDITATIONS ON FORGIVENESS

15 Minutes

Before you can forgive others, you must focus on forgiving yourself. Take a moment to think about anything that you need to forgive yourself for. As you breathe, with each exhale let go of the pain that is built up. Now, find a mirror, and tell yourself (your reflection) what you forgive yourself for, by saying "I forgive you for ...."

If you visualize an image while meditating, draw it here

15 Minutes

Think about an experience that caused you pain in the past, or an experience that is currently causing you pain. What was the cause? How have you dealt with it? (If you have a history of dismissing or minimizing your feelings, what would it mean for you to unlock that pain again? Or: If you've dealt with it head on, are there lingering feelings that you're harboring from that pain?). Take a deep breath, and as you exhale, release that negative energy by saying "I'm freeing myself of this pain" or "I release the pain this experience has caused me."

REFLECTIONS ABOUT FORGIVENESS

Think about someone who has caused your pain in the past, or who is currently causing you pain.

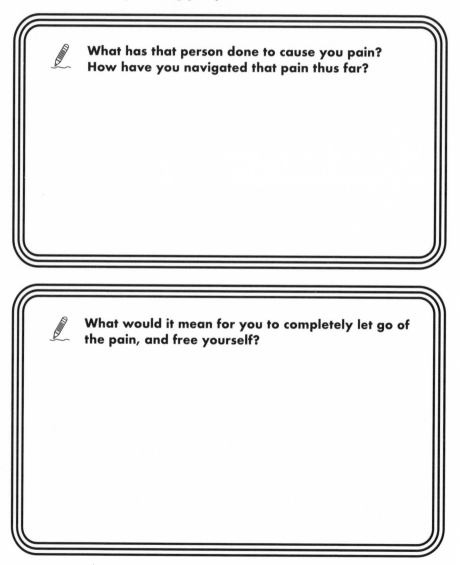

✏️ **What has that person done to cause you pain? How have you navigated that pain thus far?**

✏️ **What would it mean for you to completely let go of the pain, and free yourself?**

✏ **What steps do you need to take to fully forgive that person, and release yourself from the pain?**

✏ **What will you do to try to prevent the lasting effects of the pain from happening again?**

LIFE LESSON

SOUL-CARE

7

INTRODUCTION

Don't compromise your psychological safety. There's been a ton of debate about work-life balance, self-care, and mental health. This debate increased as people were grappling with the effects of the COVID-19 pandemic, working from home, and trying to make sense of what felt like a new normal. We've also seen an increase in people rethinking their needs and means of survival. More and more people left their jobs, particularly mothers, and rethought other aspects of their lives.

There's an international outcry for greater balance, what I like to call outcries from the soul. People are wondering about the excess that we've accumulated due to the effects of capitalism. People are also questioning racial equity, and if we can truly live in a world that values wealth over humanity. Our souls are bleeding and require critical attention.

Living in a capitalistic society, we've been conditioned to think that working hard and long hours are the key to success. We've also been conditioned to consume things at alarming rates, particularly goods that are not deemed necessary for survival. What the pandemic also allowed us to do was to slow down and rethink what's important to us, and how we operate on a daily basis. More importantly, we were forced to slow down to listen to our souls, our spirits, and our consciousness. Soul-care is akin to self-care, but it goes beyond just the surface level aspects of caring for the self. Historically, I thought that self-care meant going to get a manicure and pedicure, retail therapy, and socializing with friends. However, I was forced to rethink my understanding of self-care, and expand my inner care practices to include the soul. To take care of the soul means to consider the health of your consciousness.

There's a saying that you can't help others if you haven't helped yourself, and this is true for soul-care. When we fail to care for our souls we put ourselves at risk of health challenges. These challenges can come in the form of emotional health, mental health, physical health, social health, and even spiritual health. Many people started to rely on virtual happy hours, dance parties, and family gatherings in order to attend to their social care. I was definitely one of those people, but it wasn't enough to save me from the physical and mental health challenges that were ahead.

NOURISH YOURSELF

Prior to the start of the COVID-19 pandemic, I had a habit of neglecting to take care of my soul, as climbing the corporate ladder was something I took very seriously. While I consider myself a spiritual person, my faith was challenged at the beginning of the pandemic, and I struggled to see the light.

I was diagnosed with shingles. It took a while to figure out that stress contributed to my condition, and even my doctor was surprised that I developed shingles at my age. What he shared with me was that there are times when we become comfortable managing our day-to-day stress, despite it being unhealthy for us. We cope. He also shared that sudden and abrupt experiences could trigger reactions in the brain and body that make one susceptible to illnesses. I couldn't understand how stress from my job and the pandemic had activated such a painful viral infection in my body. However, I did reflect on how I've played a role in creating an environment for shingles to emerge. The reality is, I was guilty of putting my career ahead of my health. I was guilty of not consistently tending to my soul. I was guilty of taking care of others before I take care of myself. I was guilty of not asking for help when I first realized that I needed it.

Despite medication, the pain was unbearable, and I started to feel helpless and hopeless. I became very emotional when engaging in topics about wellbeing, work-life balance, and mental health. I continued to work, supporting my staff and graduate students through their experiences with the pandemic, but I was still neglecting my soul.

One day I decided to drive to the lake to meditate. As I was meditating my soul began to talk directly to me. I was instructed to reach out for help, something that I've always struggled to do. The first person who came to mind was my mom, and as soon as she answered the phone, she said: "Something is wrong with you, I can feel it, and I think you should consider coming home for a few weeks, just so that we can figure out as a family how to support each other through this pandemic."

I immediately began to cry because it was almost as if my spirit was speaking not only to me but also to my mother. Initially, I tried to reject her help, but my mother would not take no for an answer. What was supposed to be a two-week trip turned into a two-month trip, and that was one of the best decisions I've ever made.

While in Florida I had the opportunity to reset and rethink the things that were a priority for me. As a family, we were committed to spiritual care, exercising, cooking, meditating, and enjoying quality time with each other. Most of these I had neglected to do consistently in the past, and because of that I did not have an avenue to manage stress, as well as overcome stress.

Connecting back with family and friends has brought so much joy to my life. The battle scars on my arm are now a reminder of the wake-up call shingles gave me.

"PRACTICING SOUL-CARE ALSO MEANS TO HAVE SELF-RESPECT."

MAKING IT WORK

Stress can have a seriously negative impact on your health, and even put you at risk of an early death. When we neglect to take care of our soul, we are putting ourselves at risk and creating opportunities for stressors to take over our lives.

I've heard far too many stories of people having heart attacks and strokes because of stress. I am determined to not be one of those people. It is critical that we not only commit to taking care of our souls, but we also commit to consistency. It reminds me of the start of the New Year and how so many people fall into the trap of setting New Year Resolutions and fail to see them through. We cannot continue that pattern.

Practicing soul-care means to implement practices that enhance your psychological safety, well-being, and willpower. Practicing soul-care also means to have self-respect. The pandemic gave me time to reflect on what's important to me, and to reprioritize things in my life, such as my mental health, ultimately tending to my soul.

MEDITATIONS ON SELF-CARE

10 Minutes

Close your eyes, take a deep breath and consider your wellbeing. What are some aspects of your life that are bringing you joy? Why do those things bring you joy? Pay close attention to your breathing. Make note of the things that are bringing you joy, and be sure to acknowledge those things (e.g. spending quality time with loved ones and sharing with them that this brings you joy).

If you visualize an image while meditating, draw it here

10 Minutes

Close your eyes, and take a moment to consider what you need more of in your life. Pay attention to your breathing as you're thinking about those areas of need. Now consider, how might soul-care help you achieve those things?

REFECTIONS ABOUT SELF-CARE

Think about your current soul-care practices.

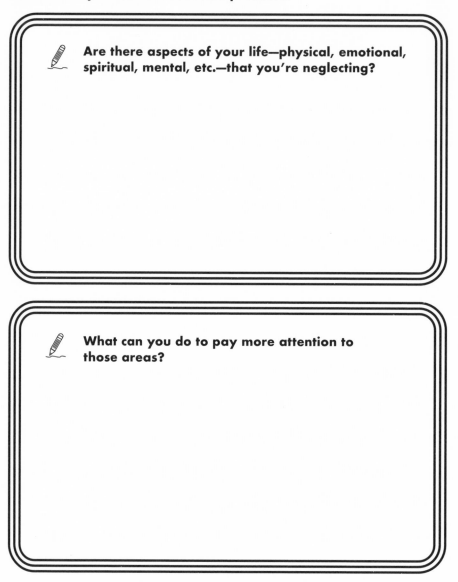

Are there aspects of your life—physical, emotional, spiritual, mental, etc.—that you're neglecting?

What can you do to pay more attention to those areas?

What commitments are you willing to make?

What sacrifices are you willing to make for your soul?

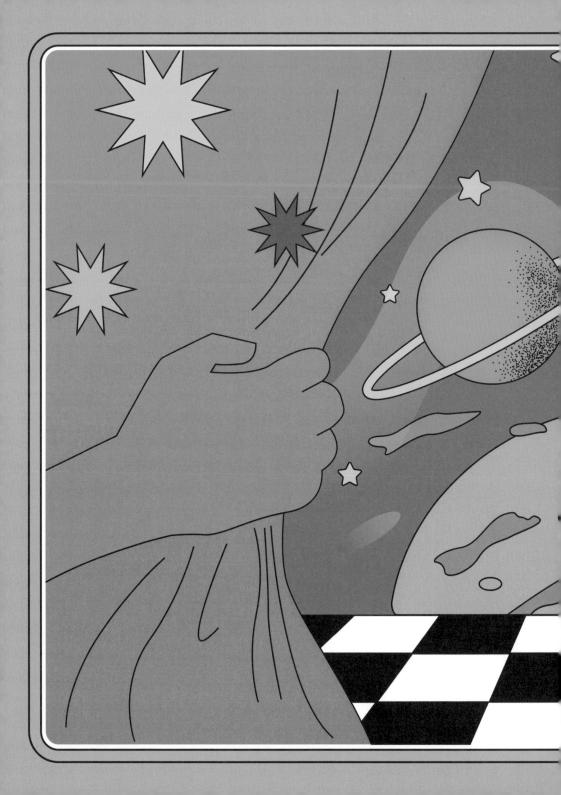

LIFE LESSON

INTEGRITY

8

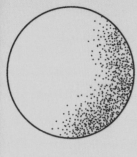

INTRODUCTION

Honesty and truth are not the same. To me, honesty means to err on the side of not telling lies. However, telling the truth means to present all the facts and an accurate representation of reality.

People often swing the pendulum between honesty and truth, allowing context and comfortability to dictate whether they go right or left. Ultimately, this can end up being a test of integrity, or an assessment of moral principles. When you lead life with a sense of integrity, you cultivate an infrastructure of principles and values and commit to leading an uncompromising adherence to those principles and values.

The battle of honesty vs. truth occurs in everyday life. We've all had times when we've chosen not to tell the whole truth—often to protect someone's feelings, or perhaps in certain circumstances where you just didn't want to share every personal detail. The decision might be well-intentioned, have low stakes and may even turn out to be the most appropriate course of action in that case. However honesty over truth might not always bring about the best outcome. Let's say that you're on a date, and the person asked you what are the qualities that you like and don't like about them. You decide to be truthful about the qualities you like, but for what you don't like, you settle on the fact that they chew very loudly. In reality, you feel that this person is more of an active talker than listener. To protect that person's feelings, you err on the side of honesty as opposed to truth. After several dates, you decide that this isn't going to work, and you communicate that to the person you're dating.

Had you told the truth from the beginning, you wouldn't end up in a situation where you're developing resentment and having to let someone down who was really interested in getting to know you. It can be hard to judge what the best way to help someone is and what effect not telling the whole truth might have. But trying to recognize when it's important to speak the truth, even when it's difficult, and especially to power, is key.

Systems, such as the criminal justice systems, political systems, and even healthcare systems have perfected the art of honesty while sacrificing integrity. These institutions and those who represent these institutions have neglected to tell the truth for years, costing the lives of innocent people. Unfortunately, there are too many examples of people representing these institutions and failing to speak truth to power.

In the justice system there's an understanding that lawyers must be honest, but surprisingly they don't have to be truthful. In a criminal case, a jury can convict someone based on the evidence presented, without actually hearing all the facts. It's worth mentioning that Black men make up the majority of prison sentences in the US. Sadly, the justice system continues to operate like the ships that carried over enslaved people during the transatlantic slave trade, carrying them into a life of bondage. We've seen countless times where unarmed Black men have died at the hands of police. These departments, designed to protect and serve, rarely tell the truth, acknowledging that they screwed up, yet again, and that racism is the cause of another unarmed Black man's death. Whether jail or death, what remains true is that we live in a system that was built to celebrate honesty over truth, where integrity hides in the shadows. We've also seen a lack of integrity in media spaces, especially with the widespread growth of social media engagement this past decade. News channels have become accustomed to distorting reality and truth, while clinging to their rights of freedom of the press.

However, the world as we know it is changing. People are tired of being tired, so are calling for elected officials to lead with integrity, to bring about a new world where truth is celebrated over honesty. When you operate with integrity, you operate free of deceit. To operate with integrity is to also tell the truth, as honesty can sometimes paint an impartial picture, which ultimately creates a window of opportunity for lies, deceit, and deception.

THE IMPACT OF TRUTH

When I entered the workforce, I noticed that people tended to air on the side of honesty rather than truth. As a teacher I've witnessed teachers share all the egregious behaviors a student displayed during a parent–teacher conference, but fail to share the intellectual capabilities of the student.

As I was entering into my fourth year of teaching, I found myself at a new school, in a new city. During summer professional development, we received our homeroom rosters and before I could get half-way through my list, I had a colleague lean over to me and say, "Ooo you got Vinil, thank God he's not in my homeroom, that boy is a mess." I probed, asking the teacher what she meant by her sentiments, and as she shared I couldn't help but think of the ongoing narrative of White teachers mischaracterizing and mislabeling Black and Brown boys. Others chimed in, one even noted that if he keeps on with his behavior, he'll end up dead like his father. There were others in the room singing the same "beware" song to each other about other Black boys as they were reviewing rosters. I felt like I was drowning in a sea of ignorance about cultural identity.

Because I didn't have the full picture of Vinil, and was still fairly novice in my understanding of child development, I took all of those narratives that were poured into me into the classroom. I started the first week off very stern with Vinil, as instructed by the more veteran teachers, and he didn't respond positively to that approach. In fact, Vinil initially started to show some of the behaviors that were described to me. I took a look at his past records, and saw that Vinil excelled academically and performed well on state standardized assessments. I was puzzled. I called his mom and asked for a meeting. We discussed his past experiences at the school, his triumphs and his challenges. His mom noted that no one had ever called her in for a "get to know you" meeting, and that she'd considered transferring Vinil to a new school due to his continuous behavior challenges, and after his previous teacher had suggested putting him on a behavioral plan. His mom also said that he responded well to a more nurturing approach, that he'd struggled since the passing of his father, and that he was really excited to finally have a Black male teacher.

I was stunned. I decided to remove the narrative about Vinil, and took a different approach. We scheduled morning check-ins to ensure that he was feeling good about starting his day, and when he started to display unfavorable behaviors, I reminded him about our agreement—that he would commit to showing up as the best version of himself. Our relationship grew stronger and stronger, and by the end of the year Vinil shared that I was not only his favorite teacher, but the one teacher he felt truly cared about him.

I've seen countless teachers label Black boys, in particular, as special needs or in need of behavior support with minimum pieces of evidence to support their claim. They may have been honest about the student's ability or behavior, but failed to tell the truth about the whole child. This is one of the reasons why there is a lack of trust in the public education system in America.

On that summer PD day, there were single stories effortlessly woven into a collective narrative about Black Boys. Those narratives fuel stereotypes that Black men battle across the world, being on constant defense of aggression and criminality, and being looked at as super predators. In the US, the unintended consequence is the school to prison pipeline—where there's a disproportionate representation of young Black and Brown boys who've been pushed out of school and into the prison system. There is a danger when we make an active choice to choose honesty over truth. This could mean altering the lives of others, and impacting their ability to achieve their fullest potential. There are too many accounts where honesty wasn't enough to save an innocent life, and truth could have meant challenging systems, laws, and structures that have oppressed certain groups of people. We can do better by telling the truth.

"TO OPERATE
WITH INTEGRITY IS
TO SPEAK TRUTH
ALWAYS, ESPECIALLY
TO POWER."

MAKING IT WORK

To operate with integrity is to create space for truth-telling, while embracing the opportunity and consequences of telling the truth. To operate with integrity is to speak truth always, especially to power.

With more truth-telling, we'll create a world where integrity is understood and normalized. This is easier said than done, and for many of us, we'll have to acknowledge that there's space for conflict to arise when telling the truth. If you are someone that tries to avoid conflicts at all cost, you may air on the side of honesty, to protect yourself. I would encourage you to think about the impact of being honest in certain situations. Think about if the information that you chose to withhold could help someone learn and grow, could prevent someone from traveling down a dark path or making the same mistake, or even could save someone's life. When we neglect to tell the truth, we also assume responsibility for that neglectful act , even if it's uncomfortable for us personally.

My recommendation is to make an effort to tell the truth, regardless of circumstances. You should make a commitment to clear your conscious of information that you've withheld in the past, even if it causes conflict or challenges someone's feelings. If we all committed to telling the truth more, we'll create a world that is more just and respectful of our similarities and differences. We'll create a world where our criminal justice system actually operates objectively and equitably. We'll create a world where a Black man will feel safe walking the street, driving to the store, buying candy, even sleeping. We'll create a world that acknowledges hurtful and harmful pasts, and make a commitment to make amends for those hurtful moments in time. We have the power to tell the truth, we must commit to wielding that power.

MEDITATIONS ON INTEGRITY

 10 Minutes

Close your eyes, and think about a moment in your life where you've been honest as opposed to telling the truth. What was that moment? What was the impact of you being honest? Do you think the outcome would have been different had you told the truth?

✎ **If you visualize an image while meditating, draw it here**

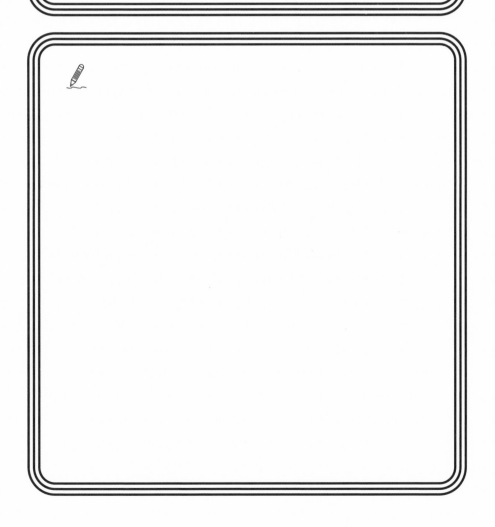

10 Minutes

Close your eyes, and think about an upcoming conversation, whether personal or professional. What would it mean for you to approach that conversation from a place of truth? What is the potential impact of telling the truth? Are you willing to commit to telling the truth?

REFLECTIONS ABOUT INTEGRITY

Reflect on another time when you were honest as opposed to telling the truth.

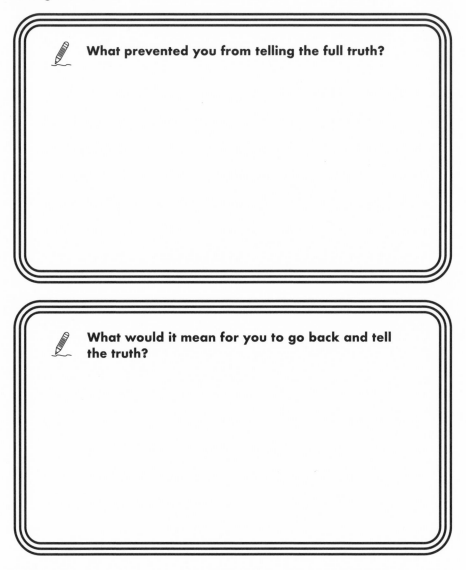

What prevented you from telling the full truth?

What would it mean for you to go back and tell the truth?

✏️ **What are some questions you can ask yourself when assessing truth over honesty?**

✏️ **How will you hold yourself accountable for telling the truth?**

LIFE LESSON

POWER

9

INTRODUCTION

Power simply means to have authority and influence over yourself and others. Regardless of your circumstances, we all have power.

Some have more power than others, given the conditions in which they grew up, their identity markers, and other social constructs such as socioeconomic status. However, we all possess power. How we use our power plays a major role in how society views us, and potential outcomes for us. There is a reason why world leaders, political figures such as civil rights activists, and entertainers, are commonly described as powerful people. Those individuals have figured out a way to harness their power for influence, oftentimes in a way that advances society or creates conditions that causes us to reevaluate how we operate as a society.

We live in a world that feels like a caste system, where people who are born into certain levels rarely move levels within the caste system. This caste system can be viewed through the lens of race, gender identity, sexual orientation, education background, even geographical location. For example, if you tell someone that you grew up in Beverly Hills, California, one might assume that you grew up wealthy, because of the notoriety that the 90210 zip code carries. If you tell someone that you grew up in Overtown, Miami, Florida, one might assume that you grew up poor, and are still poor. This argument can be applied to many facets within our society.

Educational experiences matter here as well. For example, there is a perception that people who've attended institutions such as Morehouse College, Spelman College, and Howard University are the elite of the Black educated. That perception also comes with great power and expectations of the graduates, as they are expected to go out into the world and do notable things. There's even a saying at my alma mater, Morehouse College, that states "Men of Morehouse strive to be tall enough to wear our crown of high expectations and the title of Morehouse Man." That statement alone communicates that graduates are expected to use their power to one day assume the title and crown of being a Morehouse Man.

There are some institutions, such as Morehouse, that use their power and expectations to bestow power upon you. And unfortunately, there are other institutions, like the criminal justice system, that use their power and influence to bleed you of your power. It doesn't have to be powerful institutions and systems that bless and rob us of our power. Societal pressures can also be an entity that causes us to give up power and authority over our lives. When we adhere to and reinforce societal pressures, we're also relinquishing some of our power to society.

When you've reflected on your experiences, and have determined the lessons learned from those experiences, you can use those reflections as power.

HARNESSING MY OWN POWER

There are times where you might be using your power but not seeing the results you want to see. When trying to advance my career, I kept experiencing roadblocks and barriers that were preventing me from achieving my career goals.

There were conditions, such as interpersonal and institutional racism, that I encountered along the way that were hindering my growth and development, but also tarnishing my belief in my power. I decided to change that. I had to dig deep, and realize what I was capable of. I was determined to strive for more than typical success, and create a pathway that would allow me to continuously improve myself and my community. I asked myself, "Why am I working so hard to have a seat at a table that wasn't built for me?" You may have asked yourself a similar question. The power of reflection is key here. When you've reflected on your experiences, and have determined the lessons learned from those experiences, you can use those reflections as power.

My reflections led me to redirect my power, to build my own table, and start my own consulting company, Awakening Minds. I wanted to create something that would give me absolute power, freedom, and space to innovate on cultural practices that weren't serving the needs of our growing multicultural population. Although I maintained a full-time job, I no longer had the desire to be in a position of power or authority at that job. While that opportunity eventually came, it wasn't one that required me to relinquish my power and authority over Awakening Minds. I would argue that they complimented each other and aided in my overall credibility as a practitioner. Starting off and building required tenacity and stamina, both of which were challenges for me along the journey. There were times when things were flourishing and there were times when I'd go months without a client or opportunity. I didn't give up though, because I was still proud of something that I had created.

MAKING IT WORK

One could argue that wielding power towards your own personal growth and development is a symptom of self-fulfilling prophecy, and I couldn't agree more.

When you operate in your gift or purpose, you don't have to be at the head of the table; for wherever you sit or stand, the table will shift. For too long, people have expressed their desires to have a "seat at the table." In other words, there's a perception that becoming a leader in an organization, company, or political space allows you to access and activate your powers like never before. But what if you decided to construct your own table? What if you leverage the power of purpose and power of reflection to shift an existing table towards you?

The first step here is to recognize the promise and possibility of the power we each hold, then decide how we're going to harness that power for something great. We should constantly be evaluating our lives, whether personal or professional, and assessing if our power is best utilized. We should also be constantly thinking about how we can leverage our power to healing, for peace, and for the betterment of others. Ultimately, we can wield the complexities of power to create change in our lives, to advance our lives, and to put ourselves on a path of wellbeing.

When we lose track of our power, we lose a part of ourselves. We can use our power to help us recover from traumatic experiences, we can use our willpower to bring about justice to those that have wronged us, we can use our power to advance our world by fighting for basic human rights. Ultimately, our power connects us to our purpose. We mustn't however, ever use our power to cause harm, for as greater the usage of power as greater the karma of power.

MEDITATIONS ON POWER

10 Minutes

Close your eyes, and reflect on the following question: "What does power mean to you?" Now consider: "What do you currently have power over? How does that power connect to your purpose?" Pay close attention to your breathing.

If you visualize an image while meditating, draw it here

10 Minutes

Close your eyes, and consider: "What would it mean for you to use your power to fight for social justice? How can you use your power to empower others?" Make note of what comes to mind, and monitor your breathing as you reflect on the opportunity to empower others.

REFLECTIONS ABOUT POWER

What is something that you have lost power over? What steps do you need to take to regain power?

How might you need support with those steps?

✎ **What is something that you currently have power over?**

✎ **How are you using that power to advance your life, or to bring about change?**

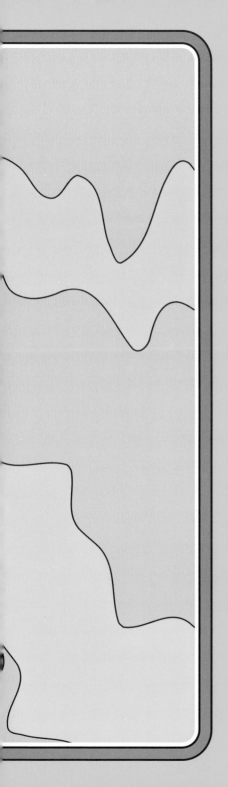

LIFE LESSON

10

PEACE, LOVE, AND LIBERATION

INTRODUCTION

A few years ago, I started signing off my emails with peace, love, and liberation.

Regardless of your circumstances, we all have power. It was a way of sharing with the person on the other end that despite the contents of the email, I wished them peace in their minds, love in their hearts, and liberation for their soul.

Every now and then people would respond by inquiring why I closed my emails the way I did, or would respond back wishing the same for me. It became my jam, the thing that I was most proud of at the end of an email. The more I wrote peace, love, and liberation, the more I started to reflect on how those concepts applied to my life, the lessons I've learned through trying to accomplish them, and the gospel I'd spread to others about them. This chapter is different from the others, as there are three concepts, or mini chapters, for us to grapple with. We'll spend time exploring each concept, and you'll have the opportunity to reflect on them individually and collectively. Finally, you'll have space to consider your own life lessons.

PEACE

I once had a debate with a close friend about peace. He asked me what is one thing that I consistently hoped for, and I responded to be at peace. He shared that he didn't believe that we could ever achieve peace, that my goal was unrealistic and too ambitious. He stated that he felt that we should aim for moments of peace in our life, and to embrace the times where we may not be at peace. I shared with him that I do think we can eventually achieve a state of peace, if we take an active role combating and blocking out the noise, stressors, and negative energy in our life that cause chaos.

To be at peace is to be in a state of quietness and tranquility, and I believe that we all can aspire to embody, and ultimately achieve peace. Having the willingness to commit and be disciplined can be a key to achieving inner peace. The reality is, we have control over how things impact us emotionally and how we react to things. If you're someone who is easily triggered, gets upset often, and allows minimal things to throw you off balance, then it may be harder for you to achieve inner peace. However, if you're someone who is moderate to strong in self-regulation then your chances of achieving inner peace is far greater. I'm not saying that if you have a short fuse that you can't achieve peace, you just have to work through those reactionary kinks while also disciplining your mind to be at peace.

LOVE

A four letter word that encompasses so many feelings and pathways. How simple a word, yet the complexity of this word is so vast. Understanding love can be complicated, and compounded by many factors. If you grew up in a loving environment, then you probably can cite your understanding of love and affection back to how you received love and affection from your family. Families modeled showing love to each other, whether it was through acts of kindness, quality time, or a simple "I love you." Many of us were taught how to love others, but very few were taught how to love ourselves. We saw our parents, grandparents, aunts, and uncles all shower their loved ones with love. Growing up in the South, family gatherings, especially during holidays, were a time for us to come together and allow the manifestation of love and happiness to commence.

What does it mean to love yourself, unconditionally? We have to pay more attention to ourselves, and recognize that our assets, accomplishments, flaws, and failures are all a product of our own doing. To love yourself unconditionally is to accept yourself for who you are, where you are in life, and where you're headed in life. In my 20s, I constantly struggled with my weight. It would fluctuate depending on stress, eating habits, exercise frequency, socializing, etc. As a result of the struggle, it was hard for me at times to look in the mirror and truly love

myself. I would spend so much time critiquing myself, and it got to a point where I didn't always like the physical being who stared back at me. This had a great impact on how I showed up in the world, especially when it came to dating.

After a series of meditation and spiritual cleansings, I decided that I could take control over my perception of myself. The reality is, I've never been skinny or a small person. I had to embrace the fact that my bones are bigger than most, that my weight wasn't going to define who I was as a person, and that I wouldn't allow my weight to prevent me from loving myself and finding love. Providing a counter narrative to situations can help save you from traveling down a dark path. My counter narrative helped me grow an appreciation for my curves, and embrace the beauty of my figure. While I'm still on my journey to fitness and health, I'm approaching it from an optimistic and loving perspective, rather than a pessimistic and degrading perspective. To love yourself is to show appreciation for yourself and the world around you. To love yourself is to see beauty through your flaws and imperfections.

LIBERATION

Many of us have experienced some form of psychological oppression that can sometimes be debilitating. For me, imposter syndrome has been, and at times, continues to be my captive. The idea of viewing yourself as not capable, not deserving, and not competent is oppressive, and inhibits the true freeing of your soul.

I grew up struggling to find someone like me, an openly gay Black man, who has a love for learning and serving. I grew up struggling with my identity as a Black man because of how my environment and media portrayed Black men. Where I'm from, we were mostly athletes and thugs. Rarely, and I mean rarely in my journey to adulthood, were there examples for me to lean on or aspire to. Even though my grandfather was one of the most loving and caring Black men I'd ever met, we still had gaps in our shared identity and our understanding of our identity. It wasn't until I got to Morehouse that I started to understand the nuances of the Black male identity, and that we too could be scholars, vulnerable, feminine, well-groomed, nurturing, and all the other qualities that don't fit the mold of the toxic Black masculinity identity.

Despite having examples in college, much of my career has been isolating. There are very few Black men in education and, as a result, I was often the only or the first in many spaces that I served. Of course there are community and social organizations, like Profound Gentlemen, that seek to bring Black men together to fellowship, learn from each other, and build meaningful connections with each other; however, my day to day has been pretty lonely. When you experience loneliness, you start to question yourself and your existence. That's how imposter syndrome became my captive. I would look around spaces, and ask myself "Why am I here? Do I deserve to be here? Am I worthy of this promotion, or speaking engagement? What if people think I'm a fraud?" Sometimes I would take myself so far down a rabbit hole that I lost sight of what I was supposed to be working on.

One day, I decided to meditate with a specific focus, freeing myself from negative thoughts that have impacted my identity. I reflected on why I am overly critical of my existence, when I've clearly proven that I deserve to be in any space that I enter. I told myself that any time doubt crept into my mind, that I would check myself by saying "I deserve to be here or I have earned this." Those simple mantras have helped me find liberation in my identity as a Black gay man. I've also been able to find freedom in my reasoning about my purpose and why I am privileged to enter spaces where I'm the only Black gay man.

"HAVE THE TOOLS TO
RESET WITH A FOCUS ON
ACHIEVING INNER PEACE ...

LOVE IN YOUR HEART FOR
YOURSELF AND OTHERS
AROUND YOU ...

FREE YOUR SOUL FROM
THE BARRIERS THAT WERE
PLACED ON YOU ..."

MAKING IT WORK

Peace

Peace can impact our functioning when we're awake. There are times when your ability to think clearly feels interrupted, or your inability to communicate clearly is prevalent, or your inability to filter through negative energy is coupled with anxiety and angst. Those are times when you should deeply reflect on your state of peace, as those are symptoms of being out of balance. My hope for you is that you continue to pursue peace, that this book has provided you with reflection opportunities that will help you achieve a greater wellbeing. I also hope that the chaos in your life is settled, that your state of wellbeing is permanent. I hope that if you ever encounter turbulence in your life, that you will have the tools to reset with a focus on achieving inner peace.

Love

My hope is that you also find love in your heart for yourself and others around you. Let's commit to embracing our flaws and imperfections. If you have the means and desire to fix them, do it because you want to do it, not because society has made you believe that you need to change. Show love to people, especially across lines of difference. One of the deficits in our world is that we don't have enough love for humankind. If we did, we'd see less suffering and disparities across the planet. One of the ways we will truly achieve equality and equity is to operate from a baseline of love, care, and kindness for each other. May love continue to manifest in the different facets of your life.

Liberation

My liberating goal for you as you read this chapter is that you free your soul from the barriers that were placed on you from birth; that you free yourself from societal pressures, and dig deep to find your passion. Question things, freely; make decisions because you want to, not because you have to. Unlock your potential by releasing the chains of doubt. Define liberation for yourself, and share it with others.

MEDITATIONS ON PEACE, LOVE, AND LIBERATION

 10 Minute Meditation

Close your eyes and think about the words "love," "peace," and "liberation" in turn. What images come to mind when you think about them? Why is that? Sit with those images in your mind, and pay attention to your breathing.

What does peace mean to you?
How do you know when you're at peace?

Do you give yourself or others more love?
Why is that?

What would it mean to live your life free
of judgment and societal pressures?

LIFE LESSON REFLECTIONS

Now you've come to the end of the book, you've had the opportunity to read about the life lessons that have shaped my soul, and I want to give you an opportunity to think about the life lessons that have shaped your life and soul. Use the space below to reflect on your own life lessons. I hope that you've found a sense of peace, love, and liberation after engaging with this book. Consider:

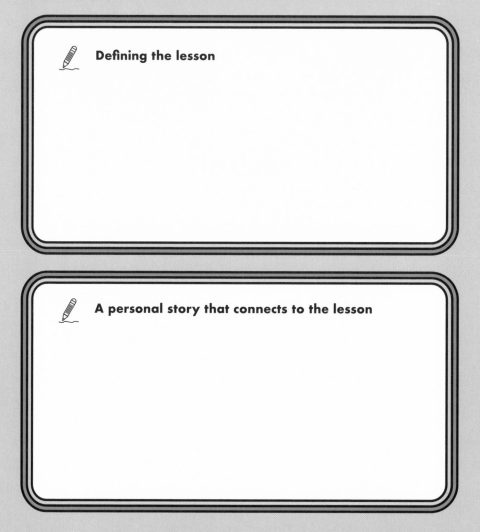

Defining the lesson

A personal story that connects to the lesson

🖊 **How might one apply that lesson to their life?**

🖊 **What questions might you ask to get someone to reflect on the life lessons you shared?**

FURTHER RESOURCES

Books

Adichie, Chimamanda Ngozi, *We Should All Be Feminists*, Fourth Estate, 2014

Alexander, Michelle, *The New Jim Crow: Mass Incarceration in the Age of Colourblindness*, Penguin, 2019

Coates, Ta-Nehisi, *Between the World and Me*, Text Publishing Company, 2015

Garza, Alicia, *The Purpose of Power*, Doubleday, 2020

Gay, Roxane, *Bad Feminist*, HarperCollins, 2014

Glaude Jr., Eddie, *Democracy in Black: How Race Still Enslaves the American Soul*, Crown Publishing Group, 2017

Hurston, Zora Neale, *Their Eyes Were Watching God*, Virago Press, 2020

Kabatt-Zinn, Jon, *Coming To Our Senses: Healing Ourselves and the World Through Mindfulness*, Piatkus, 2005

Kendi, Ibram X., *How To Be an Antiracist*, Bodley Head, 2019

Obama, Michelle, *Becoming*, Viking, 2018

Thomas, Angie, *The Hate U Give*, Walker Books, 2017

Winch, Guy, *Emotional First Aid: Healing Rejection, Guilt, Failure, and Other Everyday Hurts*, Plume Books, 2014

Podcasts

8 Black Hands: Championing discussion about the education of Black minds in America.

Black and Brown Get Down: A look at the complex nature of pop culture and race.

How To Fail With Elizabeth Day: Embracing the lessons we can learn from failure.

I Weigh with Jameela Jamil: Challenging societal norms by talking to diverse voices about their mental health.

Pod Save The People: Exploring news, culture, social justice, and politics, with a special focus on overlooked stories that often impact people of color.

The Positive Psychology Podcast: Exploring scientific insights into happiness and meaning.

Meditation Apps

Endel Meditation: endel.io

Liberate Meditation: liberatemeditation.com

ACKNOWLEDGMENTS

To the people that helped shape my lived, learned, and labored experience—thank you.

To my tribe—thank you.

To the Yoruba and Fulani people, my ancestral lineage—I am you, you are me.

This cover is for you.